The
Cruelest
Con

The True Story of A Monstrous Deception Leading to The Deaths of Two Innocent Women

By

Dr Hilary A. Nettleton

Grosvenor House
Publishing Limited

This book is published by
Grosvenor House Publishing Ltd
Link House
140 The Broadway, Tolworth, Surrey, KT6 7HT.
www.grosvenorhousepublishing.co.uk

A CIP record for this book
is available from the British Library

ISBN 978-1-83975-007-6

Contents

Introduction

At nearly 7'o'clock on the morning of Friday the 10th May 2013, two women were found close to death in a small budget hotel situated on the West Coast of Scotland, UK. Both were found bleeding profusely with horrific slash injuries to their arms. The older woman died shortly afterwards while the younger woman tragically passed away in hospital three days later after never regaining consciousness. The circumstances of their tragic deaths were initially reported by the local newspaper, the *'Greenock Telegraph'* as the possible result of the murderous act of a, as yet unknown, third party. As time progressed however, police soon confirmed that the two women had in fact ended their *own* lives in an act of familial suicide. In the 6 years since their deaths, little has been written on the details of the case and important questions remain. What was the exact chain of events that led up to such a truly sad act of desperation? What propelled two kind and caring women to end their lives in a budget hotel on the Clyde so horrifically? Who (or what) was the main instigator behind their truly tragic actions on that day? And in the same or similar circumstances, would we *all* have been taken in by the same lies and cruel deception that underpinned their actions on that day? In the end, the truth turns out to be stranger than fiction. It was a con so shockingly heartless that people could not believe the reality of what had actually happened.

This book charts the actions of the McDonough's tormentor and the complex web of lies that she wove around stories of a phantom girlfriend, a bogus pioneering stem cell trial, non-existent murdering doctors, and a fake government cover up. This book also discusses some of the more recent twists and turns that have taken place in this case since it was formally processed in a Scottish court in 2015.

Background

Mother and daughter Margaret and Nicola McDonough (aged 52 and 23 respectively at the time of their deaths) grew up in the small Scottish town of Paisley situated approximately 7 miles from the sprawling cosmopolitan City of Glasgow, UK. Nicola went to school in Paisley at St Andrew's Academy. In the month before her death, Nicola was an undergraduate student and charity worker. She had successfully completed a B.A (Hons) degree in Social Work at Paisley College of Technology (now the University of the West Coast of Scotland) and was in the process of applying for jobs. At the time of her death, Nicola had been shortlisted for at least one interview and was planning a holiday in Switzerland with three friends from university. By all accounts, Nicola's life was clearly on the 'up'. She was an intelligent, compassionate young woman with a supportive family and extremely promising future ahead of her.

Nicola's mum Margaret was as equally successful in her life. She worked as a foster carer for Renfrewshire District Council and twice stood as a Liberal Democrat candidate in local council elections. Mother of four Margaret was a strong public advocate of the rights of children and over the years, championed a whole range of issues around the protection and safety of children. In her Lib Dem campaign leaflet, Margaret emphasised that she saw 'first hand the needs of very vulnerable children in her care and their families and would like to be able to take some of that knowledge into the decision-making processes of the council'. Margaret was also a divorcee, after her 28-year marriage ended in 2008.

From research, less is known about the perpetrator of the crime, Linsey Cotton. What *is* known is that Cotton was a bar worker born on the 22 August 1982 and a single mother-of-two. She lived in Addiewell, (East Lothian), a town approximately 40 miles from where Margaret and Nicola lived in Paisley. There is no evidence that Cotton knew or had any association with either of the women prior to hatching her blackmail plot. Given the ultimate and tragic consequence of her deception, it is incredulous to think that Cotton targeted the McDonough's, initially at least, *by chance*.

Nicola and Margaret McDonough
(Image Reproduced with Permission of Spindrift)

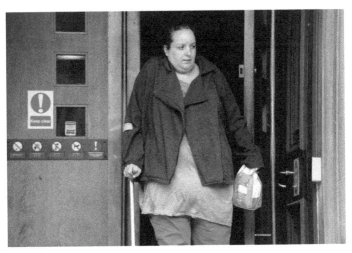

Linsey Cotton
(Image Reproduced with Permission of Spindrift)

Linsey Cotton
(Image Reproduced with Permission of Spindrift)

Linsey Cotton
(Image Reproduced with Permission of Spindrift)

Chapter 1:

Catfishing, Love Bombing
and the Con Begins

As already mentioned, there is no evidence that Linsey Cotton held any form of grudge against Margaret or Nicola McDonough or that she planned to target them directly from the outset. Nor even that financial gain was indeed Cotton's *principle* overriding motivation at the start of her con. However, her actions were clearly **not** 'spontaneous' but the result of planning by Cotton over several months. Sadly, it seems that Margaret and Nicola were drawn more deeply into her plan as Cotton's lies and deception progressed and gained pace.

The start of Linsey Cotton's plot in fact took the form of what is commonly called 'catfishing' or 'love bombing'. Both are highly manipulative practices in which someone is showered with lots of attention and affection in order to influence their behaviour and make them believe that they are in an intense relationship. 'Love bombing' as the name implies happens rapidly as the target is overwhelmed with flattery and compliments. 'Catfishing' refers to the practice of creating a fake profile in order to start an online romance. It is an inherently deceptive activity designed to carry out a particular fraud. It is often used for romance scams on dating websites.

In the case of Linsey Cotton, her main 'target' was Margaret McDonough's son Michael. Michael (then 33 years old) worked as a Corporal serving in the Royal Air Force at their military base in Lossiemouth (Moray, Scotland). In August of 2011, Michael joined the online dating website 'Plenty of Fish'. At the same time as Michael joined the website, Linsey Cotton created a fake dating profile posing as a pretty young woman called Stephanie Wilson (or Johnstone) who was a student at the University of Edinburgh. 'Stephanie Wilson' was in fact the name of Cotton's stepsister's daughter who had no idea that her photo and details were being used to perpetuate Cotton's online scam. Photos of the attractive newlywed Stephanie MacLaren (22) were used as bait to lure RAF man Michael McDonough in on the 'Plenty of Fish' website. Cotton had used her identify before to dupe unsuspecting men. The real Stephanie later told the Scottish newspaper *The Daily Record* that Cotton had 'stolen her life' by twice posing as her to con innocent men. In reality, she barely knew Linsey Cotton and had little relationship with her. She only found out that her profile was being used when a family member told her in 2011 that Cotton was using her photos on a Facebook profile under the name Stephanie Moodie. She says: *"It's just so creepy and nasty and I'm disgusted that I have been dragged into it...I didn't want people to think the profile was anything to do with me. To get the fake profile removed I had to create my own profile and then lodge a complaint about the other one."* However, none of these measures deterred Linsey Cotton.

In May 2012, Cotton messaged Michael McDonough continuing to use the alter ego of 'Steph'. Michael saw the attractive profile of 'Steph' and fell for her. They soon exchanged mobile phone numbers and began communicating with each other on a regular basis. When they began phoning each other Michael assumed that it was 'Steph' that he was talking to. Instead, it was Cotton that he was talking to and she wasted no time filling his head with lies. Very quickly Michael believed that he was in a relationship with the woman he knew as 'Steph'. It was at this stage that Linsey Cotton's cruel scam formally took shape. A key feature of this case is then how rapidly events took place between Michael McDonough and 'Steph' over a relatively short period of nearly 12 months. In this time so many lives were tragically changed and altered beyond all recognition.

The facts of the case (as cited in the *Judiciary of Scotland 2015*) are that soon after she contacted Michael McDonough (June 2012), Cotton inundated Michael with a staggering 33,369 pieces of communication. In one month alone (June 2012) there were 4,766 texts sent between Linsey Cotton and Michael McDonough. Over a 24-hour period, this averages one communication every 9 minutes. By the following month (July of 2012) this increased to an astonishing 5,756 texts. In August 2012, there were 3,263 texts noted between Michael McDonough and Cotton – an average of one contact every fourteen minutes in a period of 24 hours. This frenzy of communication intensified closer to Margaret and Nicola's death (in May 2013) when 130 texts were sent in less than six-hours. These messages were often sent late into the night.

Cotton undoubtedly used this 'flooding' or 'blitzing' technique as a conscious strategy to rapidly draw in her 'target' Michael. Importantly, it minimised the time that Michael had to actually reflect on what was happening to him and to question who the enigmatic 'Steph' really was. By ensuring that the contact taking place between them was rapid and intense- often taking place over marathon late-night conversations- Cotton also limited Michael's opportunity to share the details of what she was actually saying to him to his work colleagues, friends and family. This process of 'love bombing' is not new but is a common strategy of 'romance' frauds. Often the victims are manipulated early on in the relationship through a constant barrage of phone calls, texts and messages. In the case of Michael McDonough the effects of such aggressive storming would have been terrifying and unsettling. However, no one could have predicted that events were only to get much much worse.

Chapter 2:

The Sinister Fantasy Unfolds: Bogus Stem Cell Treatment and a Government Cover Up

Following Linsey Cotton's barrage of communication, Michael McDonough soon believed he was in a genuine romantic relationship with the enigmatic 'Steph'. Why would he not have done at this stage? 'Steph' was contacting him on a regular basis and their relationship appeared to be mutually exclusive, with no one else on the scene. However, it does seem that once Cotton was sure that she had Michael firmly 'hooked', her con took on a much more sinister form. The motive? Money combined with a desperate need for male attention.

Once in a 'relationship' with Michael, Cotton posing as 'Steph' began to weave a more complex web of lies. She used several mobile phones and laptops to invent a whole cast of characters in order to manipulate Michael and get money from him- these characters included Sammy ('Steph's mum); Billy (step brother of 'Steph'), Ashley (a nurse); QC Quentin (a barrister); and Sonia 'Steph's' sister, amongst others. Of course, none of these people actually existed but were all an elaborate fantasy created in the mind of Linsey Cotton.

Using the characters that she had created, Cotton was able, over several months, to manipulate her 'relationship' with Michael and crucially, manoeuvre him into spending his money on 'Steph'. Cotton soon began to involve herself more deeply in the fantasy she had created, convincing Michael that she was like a mother figure to 'Steph' while at the same time using her alter ego to coerce him into doing what she wanted. For example, Cotton conned Michael into buying the mysterious 'Steph' an expensive necklace for her birthday.

Cotton's lies knew no bounds and her stories lurched from the preposterous to the ridiculous. Pretending to be 'Steph', she made up the story to Michael that she was having problems with her sister's boyfriend Jason. Then, posing as 'Steph's' mum (Sammy), she said that Jason physically assaulted her daughter and that 'Steph' was left with a fractured cheek, broken arm and a broken jaw. The attack was so severe that she had also been left with a suspected fractured skull and a serious bleed on the brain. While continuing to pose as one of 'Steph's' relatives, Cotton lied that 'Steph's' injuries were so bad that she in fact had to be admitted to hospital to undergo plastic surgery.

It is at this stage in Linsey Cotton's sinister plan that she invented her most elaborate story to date- a tale pivotal to later drawing in Michael McDonough's mother and sister into her plan. Central to Cotton's story was her claim that 'Steph' could only recover from her injuries if she took part in a pioneering stem-cell trial offered by a secretive medical company called 'Biotech Scotland'. Taking part in such a trial would allegedly cure all of 'Steph's' medical problems. To make sure that Michael did not visit 'Steph' in person and hence uncover her lies, Cotton claimed that as part of her treatment, 'Steph' had to be moved around to different hospitals. Cotton also went on to create further bogus people to help dupe Michael. For example, Michael was telephoned by 'Ashley'- 'Steph's' nurse- to re-assure him that she was closely monitoring 'Steph' in hospital and that there was no need for him to visit.

Michael only met Cotton as herself for the first time when she conned him into living with her and her two children at her home in Addiewell. She did this by lying to him that it would be a better way of more closely monitoring 'Stephs' medical care. Cotton befriended Michael McDonough at this stage by claiming that she was "Stephanie's" only real-life friend who had been granted power of attorney over his fictitious girlfriend. What is important to note here is that, despite the impression that Cotton was wanting to give – of a romantic relationship between them- her relationship with Michael McDonough was purely platonic. This was not however, what Cotton wanted and she tried various 'tricks' to make her relationship with Michael more than 'friendly'. For example, on one occasion she pretended to be 'Steph' and contacted Michael to say that 'Linsey needs a cuddle' and that she should sleep with him. Remarkably he did as she suggested and slept with Linsey Cotton fully clothed but had no sexual contact with her.

Speaking in the Scottish *Daily Record* newspaper, Cotton's teenage daughter makes it clear that she had no knowledge of 'Steph' and only learned about her after reading her name in the press. From her perspective, Cotton's daughter believed that her mother and Michael McDonough were in a serious romantic relationship with one another. She states, *'my understanding was that Michael was my mum's fiancée and they had got engaged'*. She goes on, *"My mum has had boyfriends before, two or three, and they have always left her. My mum was quite scared he would leave her. My mum thought she had found someone genuinely nice and that's what me and my family thought. We thought he was a really nice man."*

The impression given that Cotton was in a close, loving relationship with Michael McDonough was reinforced when Cotton's son and daughter visited him at the RAF base he worked at. Cottons daughter says: *Michael let me and my brother and my friend go up to Lossiemouth at the RAF base.*

"We had a great time and he introduced himself to my friend as my mum's fiance. That is how we understood it. Cotton's daughter also claims that she stayed overnight at Margaret and Nicola's home in Paisley. It is not clear however, whether she actually met either of the women while she was there. Michael was also manipulated into taking Cotton and her children on holiday to Newcastle and buying an expensive pendant as a birthday present. This degree of overlap between Cotton's own family life with her children and her plan to deceive Michael McDonough, suggests that while

Cotton's main reason for her deception was money, she also craved male attention – albeit that Michael was completely duped into giving this attention to Cotton by her twisted lies and emotional manipulation.

There can also be no doubt that, as with the rest of the McDonough family, Michael was a caring individual whose only concern was for his 'girlfriend' who he believed was seriously unwell in hospital. He was expertly controlled by Linsey Cotton and rapidly drawn into her complex stories and web of lies. After only a couple of months she manipulated Michael into proposing to 'Steph' on the basis that if they were engaged, he might be allowed to see her in hospital. The RAF Corporal was so convinced by this lie that he went onto buy 'Steph' a £1,870 engagement ring after she had text him saying "*Where's my ring? If you loved me you would have bought me a ring*". Michael was so stressed at not being able to see his fiancée that he eventually left his job as a technician at the RAF base in January 2013.

Chapter 3:

Expanding the Net: Margaret and Nicola McDonough are Drawn In

Cotton's manipulation of Michael McDonough was severe on its own. However, it became much more disturbing when his mother and sister were drawn into her lies. One can surmise that, for Cotton, drawing in Margaret and Nicola McDonough at this stage was purely and simply about extorting money from them. Cotton had already taken money and goods from Michael (over the course of a year she tricked Michael out of £5000 and expensive gifts) and arguably, could have ended her fraud at that point. Instead however, she made the conscious decision to target Margaret and Nicola and this shows the brutality of her actions.

Bringing both Margaret and Nicola McDonough into her scheme took place when Cotton made up the story to Michael that 'Stephs' top secret stem-cell treatment with Biotech Scotland had taken a more sinister turn. Originally, Cotton had been careful to portray Biotech Scotland as 'Stephs' 'saviour'- her only way of receiving the expert medical care that she needed in order to cure her extensive medical problems. Cotton however, soon changed her story and lied to Michael that the Biotech trial was being infiltrated by rogue Doctors who were trying to kill all of the patients on the trial, including 'Steph'. The reason? So that the company would receive a £100 million pounds payout if all of the participants in the trial died. This was clearly an audacious fabrication on Cotton's part that made no rational sense. Why on earth would a medical company, intent on promoting its expert medical practices and services long-term, want to end the lives of all those individuals receiving medical care from that same company? Cotton embellished her story with a further claim that the British government was involved in trying to cover up the Biotech scandal and that the scandal was so big that the government had banned the press from reporting any information on the case. Again, while this story seemed preposterous, because of Cotton's proficiency in emotional exploitation and control, Michael McDonough believed the Biotech story in its entirety. Michael was convinced that Biotech was preventing him from seeing 'Steph' and that the company was ultimately trying to poison her and all of those taking part in the trial. Believing that his fiancée was genuinely in danger, Michael was duped into giving Cotton £5000 for 'Steph's' care.

Michael's mother and sister were cruelly exploited when Linsey Cotton introduced a new element to her Biotech story- the issue of a confidentiality agreement. Cotton claimed that 'Steph's' stem-cell treatment was the subject of a (non existent) confidentiality agreement. This meant that Michael McDonough, as the main focus of this confidentiality agreement, was expressly forbidden from discussing any details of 'Steph's' case with his friends or family members. However, Michael was clearly under a lot of pressure at this time and, in a vulnerable state and needing the support of his family, told his mother Margaret (who in turn told her daughter Nicola) about his 'girlfriends' desperate situation. Margaret and Nicola were naturally extremely worried about what was happening to their son and brother respectively and wanted to help him.

It was at this time around the non-existent confidentiality agreement that Cotton's cruelty and lies gained a new momentum. When Michael told his mum and sister about the situation with 'Steph' and Biotech Scotland, Cotton saw a prime opportunity to make more money. After telling Michael McDonough that she knew the confidentiality clause had been breached, Cotton made her boldest move yet: she actually went to the family home of Margaret and Nicola McDonough in Paisley (on 7th April 2013) and confronted both of the women. Cotton- pretending to be 'Steph's' friend- told a very frightened Margaret and Nicola that they could face a long prison sentence of 20 years because they had breached a confidentiality clause relating to 'Steph's' medical treatment. The swindler claimed she knew a lawyer who could make the case disappear for £7,000. Cotton also claimed she could obtain a false passport for £700, which would mean that Nicola could leave the country. This whole story was, of course, pure fiction and the product of Linsey Cotton's warped imagination. However, it was a wicked and cruel deception that put in motion a horrendous series of tragic events for the whole of the McDonough family.

Linsey Cotton
(Image Reproduced with Permission of Spindrift)

Linsey Cotton
(Image Reproduced with Permission of Spindrift)

Chapter 4:

Deathly Fear: Crisis Point for Nicola and Margaret McDonough

After visiting Margaret and Nicola McDonough at their home in Paisley in 2013, Cotton ramped up her lies. She made the claim that 'Steph' could only be saved from the Biotech scandal with support from the European Court of Human Rights. Cotton convinced Margaret and Nicola that if they both provided testimonies, these would support a case to the European Court. Michael's mum and sister duly agreed to provide written testimony supporting how badly Michael had been affected by the treatment that his girlfriend 'Steph' had received at the hands of Biotech Scotland.

Cotton, later posing as a lawyer, began sending Margaret and Nicola threatening messages claiming that they would only be safe if they left Scotland and moved away. Nicola and Margaret were obviously terrified that they would be imprisoned or even killed by the government. Nicola was hysterical and was physically sick. Both women believed all of Cotton's lies and what she was telling them about the importance of a potential European Court case.

Despite the obvious terror and distress that she was causing to Nicola and Margaret McDonough, Cotton did not stop but ramped up her manipulation and lies. She continued to put pressure on Michael's sister Nicola to provide a written testimony to the European Court of Human Rights, outlining the effect that the Biotech trials had on her brother. However, Nicola was terrified when she received a letter, allegedly from 'Steph' letting her know her that her testimony was 'not good enough'. The letter went on to say that:

"Your big brother has asked you for help and it has become apparent you could not be bothered to give it a go. Enjoy your life Nicola while I struggle with mine"

Cotton was adamant that Nicola and Margaret McDonough should be 'punished' for their alleged non co-operation. In text messages to 'Steph', Michael also claimed that he could never forgive his family for breaching the confidentiality clause. Further pitting son against mother, Cotton (posing as 'Steph') said of Margaret McDonough: "*She fucking new full well what she was doing. I can't forgive your mum and I want your sister to be punished. That bitch cannot be trusted and she thinks nothing of destroying people's lives. Inside she's a mess*".

Of course, there was no secret stem-cell treatment, no confidentiality clause and no European Court case. It was all a scam dreamed up by Cotton in order to manipulate the McDonough family. 'Steph' – in reality Cotton- would work on Michael in long late night conversations, threatening to end their relationship if he did not do what she wanted him to do.

The agreed Crown narrative on what happened at this point confirms the following facts of the case:

"On the 7th of April 2013, the accused and Michael (McDonough) had a meeting with Nicola McDonough at the family home to decide what was to happen at the European Court. Nicola McDonough was not happy about attending court, but she agreed to go to a court date planned for 24 April 2013

'About this time, Matthew McDonough (brother of Michael) witnessed Nicola McDonough in hysterics and crying because she believed that her statement had caused problems for Michael"

On the 6th of May 2013, texts were sent from Linsey Cotton to Michael McDonough to put further pressure on the McDonough family:

From Cotton to Michael *'...And I want revenge on ur stupid f***ing sister...I want to put her in f***ing prison she opened her f***ing mouth!!'.*

From Cotton (posing as the lawyer Callum) to Michael *'...They have just stated that if Linsey is not to be held accountable it will have to be both your mum and Nicola that go to prison instead'.*

The dreadful consequences of all of the above lies were laid out at the start of this book. Namely, that on the evening of Thursday 9th May 2013, Nicola and Margaret McDonough drove 17 miles from their home in Paisley to the Premier Inn in Greenock. They arrived at the hotel at 3.50pm in Mrs McDonough's red Suzuki. They then left to go out a short time later and returned to the hotel in Greenock between 12.30am and 1am the next day. Police suspected that the women had spent hours visiting chemists as far away as Balloch (Dunbartonshire) 35 miles away. Their absence from their hometown had not gone un-noticed, however, as the pair was reported missing 17 hours before they were discovered at the Premier Inn. The alarm was raised when Mrs McDonough did not turn up at nursery to collect her foster son.

The horrific discovery of the bloodied bodies of Nicola and Margaret took place at just after 7am on Friday 10th May 2013. Margaret was found dead in a bedroom with deep slash wounds to her arms. Her daughter was found unconscious in the upstairs corridor of the hotel with serious cutting wounds to her neck and arms. Nicola survived for only 72 hours and died in hospital before police could question her over what had happened. From the beginning, Scottish Police insisted that they were not looking for a third party.

The Premier Inn, Greenock
(Image Reproduced with Permission of Spindrift)

Police Car at Premier Inn
(Image Reproduced with Permission of Spindrift)

The Premier Inn where both women died
(Image Reproduced with Permission of Spindrift)

The Premier Inn on the Clyde
(Image Reproduced with Permission of Spindrift)

Inverclyde Hospital, Greenock where
Nicola later passed away
(Image Reproduced with Permission of Spindrift)

Nicola McDonough
(Image Reproduced with Permission of Spindrift)

Nicola McDonough
(Image Reproduced with Permission of Spindrift)

Death certificates that were issued later on formally recorded that Nicola died on May 13th at Glasgow Royal Infirmary and her mother on May 10th. Forensic pathologist Dr Julia Bell recorded the main cause of death as "incised wounds to the left arm" (for Margaret) and Nicola's was a single wound to the left arm. No mention was made of claims in the media that both women had overdosed on paracetamol.

On the 13th June 2013, a requiem mass, attended by hundreds of mourners, was held at St Mirin's Cathedral in their hometown of Paisley. At the end of the service Margaret's coffin was carried out of the Cathedral by her sons Mathew (then 20 years old) and Micheal (then aged 31). Nicola's coffin was carried out by her father Tom and brother Kevin. Both women were then given a private burial at Hawkhead Cemetery in Paisley.

Further details that came out in the days following their deaths showed that on the day before she was found dead (May 9th), Margaret McDonough had made out a will at MSM Solicitors in Paisley. In her will, Mrs McDonough's job was listed as foster carer and she signed it in the presence of a partner at the firm. Margaret instructed that her estate, made up of the family home in Paisley and valued at £254,509, should be left to her three sons. Daughter Nicola was not mentioned in the will and her eldest brother (Kevin) was appointed executor of their mother's estate. Excluding Nicola from her will seems to be a strong indicator that Margaret already knew of the suicide pact between herself and her daughter and so was not concerned about excluding Nicola from her share of the assets of her will.

Margaret McDonough's brother William said the deaths remain a mystery. He said: *"Margaret and Nicola were always very caring and cheerful. They were best friends and always out together. Margaret had just adopted a wee boy and had just bought a jacket for him the week before for starting school. I'm very upset. I can't really understand it."*

Chapter 5:

The Net Closes In, Trial, and Sentencing

Nearly 10 days after Nicola and Margaret were found at the Premier Inn in Greenock, Linsey Cotton's reign of cruelty and manipulation was finally discovered.

It was only following the deaths of Margaret and Nicola McDonough that Cotton's name was linked to the family. On May 22nd (2013), police officers in Scotland visited Cotton at her home to ask questions about the deaths of the two women. After searching Cotton's house, police found most of the equipment that she had been using to carry out her crime. It included 15 mobile phones, two laptops and two tablets. Through careful forensic investigation of these items, it was found that all of these devices had been used to dupe the McDonough's into believing that they were in contact with more than 12 different people. It was a heinous crime had cost the lives of two innocent women.

At a pre trial hearing, Cotton initially denied all of the charges against her. She denied repeatedly contacting Michael McDonough using the phony profile of 'Steph' and pretending to him and his family that he was in a relationship with the non-existent woman. She also pleaded not guilty to repeatedly pretending to Michael and his family that 'Steph' was seriously injured and needed treatment from a drug company called Biotech Scotland. Cotton further denied trying to extort thousands of pounds from former Liberal Democratic Candidate Margaret and her daughter. Cotton also rejected the charge that she had attempted to defeat the ends of justice by deleting electronic data on the mobile phones that police had found and getting rid of paperwork. It is also alleged (which Cotton denied) that Cotton had tried to manipulate Michael into helping her destroy evidence and provide false accounts of events in order to ensure that her crime would not be detected.

It is a sign of Cotton's cruel personality that she initially denied all of the charges against her. While it was in no doubt about what Cotton had done to the McDonough family, it appears that she felt little real remorse for her conduct and was reluctant to accept responsibility for the fact that as a direct result of her actions, two innocent women were now dead.

Given the seriousness of the crime, the presiding judge (Sheriff Robert Fife) initially considered referring the case to the High Court in Scotland in order to secure a potentially longer custodial sentence. However, after considering all aspects of the charges against Linsey Cotton, Sheriff Fife concluded that he had sufficient powers as a Sheriff to impose a long sentence on Cotton. The initial plan was also that Cotton's case would be heard over a four-week time period- starting October

2015. Almost 150 witnesses were also listed to give evidence in the trial, including Cotton's own son and daughter who were only 11 and 15 years old at the time of the court case.

However, in the face of the huge amount of evidence against her and no doubt on the advice of her defense Counsel Gerry Bann, Cotton eventually pleaded guilty to obtaining money, goods and services by fraud; attempted extortion; and attempting to defeat the ends of justice. Due to the fact that Cotton pled guilty, all of the witnesses that were scheduled to give evidence were no longer required to attend court.

Linsey Cotton's lawyer attempted to mitigate on her behalf, claiming that his client felt "remorse and shame for the upset and anguish her deplorable conduct caused the family". He went on to say that, "She previously indicated to me she felt sick to the pit of her stomach by what she had done. That, I would submit, is an entirely appropriate response and indicative of the remorse she feels for her dreadful behaviour".

Arguably Cotton's defense lawyer also tried to court sympathy on her behalf:

"She was assessed as being a lonely, socially isolated, needy and unhappy woman who has lost control of her weight and has absolutely no self-esteem in her ability to attain or attract a suitable partner as a result."

He said Cotton left school early because she was bullied over her size and weight. This allegedly had a serious effect on her personality and self-esteem. He also said she was assessed as suffering from "chronic anxiety" due to her image issues, and Post Traumatic Stress Disorder following the death of her father in 2004. In mitigation, Cottons defense counsel said that Cotton found it easier to live in a fantasy world she had created than deal with the realities of being her actual self.

Defence Counsel Gerry Bann said there was "no excuse for such dreadful behaviour" but said she had "loved Michael McDonough and was obsessed with him" and her lies had got more and more "far-fetched" in a bid to keep hold of Michael as she "couldn't bear the prospect of living without" him. And she said her primary motive was the relationship with Michael while "a better standard of living and finances" was secondary to that.

Bann asked for leniency for his client, saying she had been left with emotional scars after suffering violence at the hands of a series of former partners.

But Sheriff Fife ruled there was "only one appropriate sentence" and locked Cotton up for what he termed "wholly unjustified and wholly unjustifiable" conduct which would be "condemned by any reasonable person."

Cotton's mitigating circumstances- around her weight and issues of self esteem- may be genuine. All indicators are however, that throughout the court trial, Cotton still failed to fully comprehend the seriousness of her behaviour. By claiming in court that her main reason for committing the crime was that she wanted a relationship with Michael, Cotton seemed to distance herself from the malicious, cruel, and spiteful motivations behind her actions.

So while the need for male attention may have been a very small part of the reason for Cotton's scheming, it is clear that money was a powerful motivating factor. Cotton had purposively planned her deception and gained financially from keeping her lies going for nearly a year. She never detracted from her plan even though there were numerous opportunities for her to stop her deception.

Taking account of her guilty plea before the trial and her alleged expression of remorse, Cotton was sentenced to 3 years in prison. Her prison sentence was backdated to September 17th 2015- the date that Cotton was first remanded in custody.

On sentencing her at Paisley Sheriff Court, Sheriff Robert Fife made a damming statement on Cotton's crime that is worth quoting in full here:

"The agreed crown narrative discloses an extraordinary, complex and intricate web of deceit and lies. This agreed narrative of the background facts discloses a wicked course of conduct, a course of controlling and manipulative behaviour. While through your solicitor and within the Criminal Justice Social Work Report you have expressed remorse for your actions (but I have noted the comment of the author of the report on page 5 of the report of their impression that the expression of remorse was superficial), and I will take that into account in any sentence, your solicitor correctly described your conduct

at the last hearing on 17 September 2015 as 'deplorable' and today as 'dreadful'. I would reinforce that – I would describe your conduct as deplorable, callous, despicable and shameful.

On reflection about the whole circumstances of this case, I think the best word to sum up what you have done is the word 'cruel'. The word cruel means 'wilfully causing pain or suffering to others, and feeling no concern about it'.

In my view you were cruel to Michael McDonough, to Margaret McDonough and to Nicola McDonough. My sympathies go out to the McDonough family and friends for their terrible loss, but it is important that I record you have not been prosecuted for the deaths of either Margaret McDonough nor Nicola McDonough and my task today is to sentence you on the charge to which you have pled guilty.

I reject any suggestion from the psychological reports before the court that you were being 'spontaneous'. That is inconsistent with the agreed narrative of the facts. It is the extraordinary demands that you made on persons who were vulnerable: Michael McDonough, Kevin McDonough, Margaret McDonough (sadly, now deceased) and Nicola McDonough (also sadly, now deceased) that are of the gravest concern to this court"

You invented, you created fictitious persons, not just the false online dating profile and persona in the name of a Stephanie Wilson or Johnstone – no, you created a series of fictitious persons to dupe the McDonoughs.

Your false threats that Margaret McDonough and Nicola McDonough would be imprisoned for 20 years should be condemned by any reasonable person. It is clear from the terms of the agreed crown narrative that you were determined both Margaret McDonough and Nicola McDonough should be 'punished' – you wanted both of them 'out of the way' no matter what it took to do that"

Sheriff Fife went on to conclude:

"This was in my view a very serious crime. Members of the public would rightly be appalled at your conduct. The nature of the offence involved significant and continuing planning; you deliberately targeted persons who were vulnerable; you exerted pressure and influence over persons who were vulnerable; and the fraudulent activity was conducted by you over a sustained period of time".

Cotton's own mother Isabel Wilson (64) claimed that she had no idea about her daughter's scheming and that her crime had caused a major rift in the family. The first that Isabel knew of her daughter's involvement in the double suicide was when police arrested her. She says: *"She wouldn't tell me what she had done. She still won't talk about it to this day. She just says, 'Don't ask me anything, I've made a big mistake. She's never explained any of it to me. Linsey told her kids that she had been looking for happiness"*

Cotton's so-called desire for a happy relationship seems to coincide with the fact that her mother genuinely believed that Linsey was in a relationship with RAF man Michael. She said: *"I thought she had met somebody wonderful. They seemed to be in a great relationship and spent every leave he had from the RAF together and I got to know him and his son very well. They went to Lossiemouth on holiday. They looked like a wee family. I thought they were engaged and I did see a ring, a white-diamond square."*

In her interview with the Scottish newspaper *The Daily Record* Cotton's mother also revealed that her daughter was actually living with Michael McDonough when the horrific news came through that his mum and sister had been found fatally wounded in a hotel. Most shockingly Isabel Wilson told reporters that Cotton and Michael McDonough were at the hospital **together** when Michael's sister Nicola was transported there: *"Michael was devastated. Linsey seemed shocked and upset too. At this point, Nicola was still clinging to life. The two of them later came home and he was in such a bad way I made him go to the doctor".* In hospital Nicola clung to life for another three days before passing away. It shows the extent of Cotton's cruel personality that she was able to go to the hospital with Michael, comfort him and feign upset, while actually knowing that **she** was the one whose actions had directly led to Margaret and Nicola's deaths.

Despite her initial reluctance to believe that her daughter could be capable of such cruelty Cotton's mother soon realized that her own daughter was indeed guilty of a crime beyond her comprehension: *"I'm mortified. People believe Linsey's evil. We had no idea of this and I will never understand what she's done. People are shouting 'murderer' at my grandchildren in the street. I'm in total shock that I have a family member that could do something like this. I'll never get my head around it,"* Wilson told a Sunday newspaper. She also said of her daughter: *"Clearly, there are mental health issues. She's done wrong and deserves to be punished. I can never forgive her"*.

Following Cotton's sentencing in court, members of the McDonough family thanked police and the Crown Office for their professionalism and dedication "in bringing this evil individual to justice". Detective Inspector David Wagstaff officer in charge of the inquiry, said: *"This was a unique, protracted and challenging inquiry. I am relieved that the McDonough family have been spared the ordeal of a trial. The McDonough family are a loving caring family, as a result of their care and compassion Linsey Cotton was able to manipulate them and dupe them into believing her elaborate and evil lies over a 12 month period. The McDonough family have remained dignified throughout this terrible ordeal and my thoughts remain with them."*

Con women Linsey Cotton Attending Court
(Image Reproduced with Permission of Spindrift)

Linsey Cotton Attending Court
(Image Reproduced with Permission of Spindrift)

Con women Linsey Cotton
(Image Reproduced with Permission of Spindrift)

Con women Linsey Cotton
(Image Reproduced with Permission of Spindrift)

Con women Linsey Cotton
(Image Reproduced with Permission of Spindrift)

Chapter 6:

The Complex Question of Criminal & Moral Responsibility

A key question raised in the Linsey Cotton case is how responsible she actually was for the deaths of Nicola and Margaret McDonough. She was not physically in the room in Greenock when they died nor did she wield the sharp instrument that caused their fatal injuries. So should she have been charged with their deaths?

In terms of her *criminal* responsibility, Linsey Cotton was **not** charged with murder or culpable homicide but with fraud and other crimes of dishonesty. In Scotland the charge of **murder** takes place when the accused has acted with the intention of killing the victim or where the conduct of the accused has been 'wickedly reckless'. The specific offence of **culpable homicide** in Scots law means that the accused has caused the loss of life through wrongful conduct- but where there was no intention to kill or 'wicked recklessness'. Culpable homicide is a lesser charge than murder and is similar to the offence of manslaughter in English law. Culpable homicide only becomes murder when the criminal act is done squarely with the purpose of causing deaths. In

Scotland it is the Crown Office and the Procurator Fiscal Service who decide if there is enough evidence to prosecute any case in a Scottish court. The fact that Cotton was neither charged with murder nor culpable homicide in Margaret and Nicola's deaths was clearly a decision taken by the Procurator Fiscal Service. This decision was most likely taken on the basis that there was not enough sufficient evidence in the case to prove the 'intention to kill' legal proviso.

In 2013 Linsey Cotton was remanded in custody at Paisley Sheriff Court after pleading guilty to obtaining money by fraud and threatening Margaret and Nicola McDonough before their deaths. She was eventually found guilty and jailed for three years. So, Cotton was never charged in relation to the deaths of the mother and daughter but the crucial question is: should she have been?

Nicola and Margaret were so terrified at the prospect of spending their lives in prison that they slashed their wrists and ended their own lives rather than go to prison. They took Linsey Cotton's threats as real and true and sought what they thought was their only way out. The key question is how far and to what extent Cotton could have anticipated that, through her actions, the two women would go on to kill themselves? Could Linsey Cotton have reasonably foreseen that Nicola and Margaret McDonough were so vulnerable and frightened by her threats that they would end their own lives rather than face (what they thought) was a substantial prison sentence?

In terms of her strict **criminal** responsibility under the law, it is clear that Cotton could not be charged with the murder of Nicola and Margaret McDonough. This is because, according to the evidence, she had no clear intention to end the lives of both of the woman nor could she have reasonably foreseen that her actions would directly lead to their deaths. She had no direct involvement in their deaths – she was not physically present at the hotel when they killed themselves nor did she attack the women with the sharp instrument that ended their lives.

But what about Cotton's **moral** responsibility for their deaths? Moral responsibility means being ethically responsible for having done something that has led to negative consequences. In all likelihood, Cotton could not have predicted that Nicola and Margaret would have ended their lives because of her threats. However, their deaths were clearly a direct consequence of her actions. Would Nicola and Margaret have killed themselves *without* Cotton's threats? In the view of this author: more than likely, probably not. Linsey Cotton's actions (and those alone) were the sole motivators for their actions.

The whole issue of 'moral responsibility' for criminal behaviour was brought to the fore in a recent high profile case in the United States. The Sky Crime programme 'I Love You, Now Die' tells the extraordinary true story of two teenagers named Michelle Carter and Conrad Roy. They met in 2012 and carried out a relationship based on thousands of text messages before 18 year-old Roy committed suicide in July 2014. Roy had suffered with depression for a number of years and was on anti-depressants. In the months leading to his suicide in July 2014 he received a number of texts from Michelle Carter apparently encouraging him to take his own life and suggesting methods of doing it. ("Drink bleach." "Hang yourself jump off a building stab yourself idk theres lots of ways.") She also appeared to encourage him not to keep putting things off. ("You keeping over thinking it … You just have to do it like you said.") She even seemed to position herself as someone who could benefit from the attention that would be given to Roy's death. ("If you're gonna do a last tweet can it be about me."). Even at the point at which Conrad Roy got out of his carbon minoxcide fuelled car and appeared to hesitate in his plan to commit suicide, Carter ordered him over the phone to 'get back in the car' and finish the deed.

Those prosecuting Michelle Carter concluded that, through her words and verbal encouragement, Carter was morally responsible for Conrad's death. It was also decided that she was criminally responsible for the young mans death: leading as it did to her conviction for involuntary manslaughter. This meant that Carter's words and speech were seen as equaling violence under the law. She was not present when he died but the court judged that without her words of encouragement, Roy would not have died when he did. It was considered irrelevant by the court that Conrad was depressed and may have taken his life at a later date.

The Michelle Carter ruling in the USA shares many similarities with the Linsey Cotton case when assessing her culpability in the deaths of Nicola and Margaret McDonough.

Both cases highlight the complexity in apportioning criminal responsibility for death/s where (1) the defendant did not inflict any wounds or injuries on the victims and (2) was not physically present at the point of their deaths and (3) words or speech were the main source of attack. Interestingly in the case of Michelle Carter, she was charged in the USA to be both *criminally* and *morally* responsible for Conrad's death. By contrast, Linsey Cotton was only charged with fraud and received a relatively light sentence of 3 years in prison.

The fact that Linsey Cotton was neither charged with murder nor culpable homicide does not mean that Cotton should not be held as morally responsible for their deaths. She *unintentionally* caused their deaths and her behaviour was indeed reckless. Nicola and Margaret would **not** have killed themselves at the time that they did without Cotton's threats. Whether they chose to kill themselves at a later date, is immaterial to the case.

Chapter 7:

Postscript & Final Twist in the Story

A final twist in the devastating story of the McDonough family came only 6 months after sentencing when, in March 2016, Linsey Cotton (33) was found seriously ill in her cell at HM Prison Edinburgh. She was transported from the prison to Edinburgh Royal Infirmary but died on 20th March at 3.30am in the Combined Assessment Unit at the Infirmary.

Due to the fact that Cotton's death occurred while she was in legal custody, an inquiry into her death was formally instigated. Following the fatal accident inquiry at Edinburgh Sheriff Court, Sheriff Alison Stirling ruled that Cotton died as the result of from pulmonary thrombo-embolism- deep vein thrombosis of the right calf. It was stated that acute cervicitis and obesity may have been contributory risk factors for her developing thrombo-embolism. She ruled that the pulmonary embolism occurred "suddenly and without warning" and there were no reasonable precautions that could have been taken by prison or medical staff to prevent Cotton's death. On the morning of her death, staff at the Combined Assessment Unit had attempted to resuscitate Linsey Cotton for 32 minutes following a cardiac arrest but she failed to respond. Following discussion with all medical staff present, the decision was taken that any further continued measures would be futile. Resuscitation stopped at 3.10 am and Cotton's life was pronounced extinct at 3.30 am on 20 March 2016.

Issuing her judgement, Sheriff Stirling said that: "Although Ms Cotton was a young woman, she had a number of significant health issues." She suffered from obesity, type 2 diabetes, gout, menorrhagia, hypothyroidism, asthma, chronic pain and anxiety. She had had deep vein thrombosis during pregnancy in 1999 and frequently suffered from breathlessness in the weeks before she died.

Cotton was only 6 months into her 3-year prison sentence for her crimes against the McDonough's when she died.

Chapter 8:

Conmen and Woman: UK Cases & The Psychology Behind them

The story of the wicked deception inflicted on the McDonough family– and the devastating consequences of Linsey Cotton's actions- seem the stuff of fiction and Hollywood movies. The tale she spun seems incredulous and hard to comprehend- especially by those who have never been the victim of the actions of a cruel fraudster. Margaret and Nicola McDonough had no reason to doubt what Linsey Cotton was telling them about the mysterious 'Steph', her illness and her relationship with their son and brother. What is clear is that the two woman were so incredibly terrified by the position that they believed they were in, that they felt the only option available to them was to end their own lives.

Further research for this book has uncovered that Linsey Cotton was in fact not new to conning people but had a track record of committing similar deceptions. Following newspaper reports of what had happened to the McDonough's, an ex-partner of Cotton spoke up to say that he was put on anti-depressants, self-harmed and was also driven to the brink of suicide by "her warped mind games". Speaking in *The Sunday Post*, 41-year-old

Gordon Johnstone revealed that Cotton scammed him in ways scarily similar to that of the McDonough's.

Two years before her scam began with the McDonough's Cotton used the fake identity of a woman called 'Steph' to lure Johnstone into a relationship. She showed him a picture of "a very attractive girl" who he soon believed that he was receiving as many as 250 texts a week from. The texts were of course from Cotton posing as 'Steph'. As Johnstone claims *"Obviously I now know Steph' was a figment of Linsey's imagination."* Every time that Johnstone asked to meet up with 'Steph', she made up excuses. Instead of meeting up with Johnstone at the outset and pretending to be 'Steph' (which she could not have done anyway as they bore no physical resemblance to each other), 'Steph' simply told Johnstone to visit her 'Aunty' Linsey (Cotton).

To make sure that she could avoid 'Steph' meeting up with Johnstone, Cotton portrayed 'Steph' as a vulnerable young woman with lots of family problems and who led a hectic lifestyle. The reality of course was that Cotton was using these meetings with Gordon Johnstone to form a relationship with him herself.

Almost a month into his arm's length courting of 'Steph', Johnstone received a bombshell call from Cotton – in the early hours of the morning- asking him to go to her house straight away. When he arrived Cotton told him that 'Steph' had been involved in a near fatal car crash and was in intensive care at Wishaw General Hospital. When he asked, to visit her, Cotton lied that only "immediate family were allowed to visit". Eventually, Cotton used this elaborate plot to progress her relationship with Gordon Johnstone. She lied to him that she was pregnant and later, claimed that she was a gun-runner/drug courier for a Glasgow gangster. After telling Johnstone that he could be a target for these gangsters, Cotton began locking Gordon in the house whenever she went out to work, for his 'safety'. Frustrated, he would bang the floor to alert a neighbour who had a key to let him out. If the neighbours were out, Gordon would often climb out the window of the upstairs flat.

When Johnstone threatened to end the relationship with Cotton, she lied that she was suffering from breast cancer and that her daughter had leukaemia. Due to Cotton's lies, Johnstone says that he was so overwhelmed that he considered ending it all, saying: "*She is a tornado of destruction and the court case shows what she is capable of. I know how far she can push you*". Mr Johnstone goes on: "*Because of her I went from a lively outgoing guy to a paranoid wreck afraid of my own shadow. I considered ending it all too. It was only by telling my family and doctors I needed help that I was able to stay strong*" Gordon Johnstone was put on anti-depressants as a result of Cotton's actions. Pointedly he claims: "*I know what poor Margaret and Nicola would have felt like — people wouldn't believe what she is capable of.*"

While Gordon Johnstone was clearly a victim of Linsey Cotton's lies and deception, arguably so too was her neice Stephanie MacLaren whose online identity Cotton used to trap unsuspecting men. The real Stephanie only became aware Cotton was up to her old tricks again after Margaret and Nicola McDonough died in May 2013. Police visited Cotton's neice at her home and were initially suspicious that she might be an accomplice in her aunt's con, *"They took away my mobile phone and computer IP details. I was shocked when I realized that they were somehow connecting me to their deaths"*. She goes on, *"They were firing names at me but it was soon obvious I didn't know what they were talking about. They did say that if she was using my photograph it was because I was young. The next thing I knew I was getting summoned for court appearances"*. Cotton's family and friends were adamant in their talks with the police that they knew nothing about her scheming. A family member said Cotton, *"was obsessed with dating and spent her time on the computer with her fantasies, which obviously turned into something really sinister."* The reality was that none of her family actually knew the full extent of her scheming online. Cotton, operating **alone** was the sole designer of her warped plan to con Michael McDonough and his mother and sister.

Gordon Johnstone's experience of Linsey Cotton shares some key similarities with those of the McDonough family-: the allusive, then seriously ill fictitious girlfriend; the expert manipulation and lies designed to extort money; the barrage of phone calls and text messages; the desperate need for attention; and the incredulous tales of tragedy, intrigue and mystery. This begs an important question: under similar circumstances and with similar lies being told would we *all* have fallen victim to the same or similar con? Are there common features of such cons that draw victims in?

The way in which the McDonough family was cruelly manipulated by Linsey Cotton, is, sadly, not an isolated case. Instead, there have been a number of cases where people of all ages and social backgrounds have become victims of the actions of cruel conmen and women. Many have been manipulated into having relationships with people who are rarely who they profess to be and who go onto con them out of huge sums of money. In other cases (eg. the case of Juliette D'Souza discussed below) there is no romantic interest to the con but the deception is all about stealing as much money as possible money from the victim/s.

Robert Hendy-Freegard

Robert Hendy-Freegard was widely reported in the UK media because of the bizarre lies he told and the large numbers of victims involved. Hendy-Freegard was an experienced conman whose life was based upon a fantasy world that he had created of fast cars, beautiful girlfriends and a bogus career in MI5. He posed as a James Bond style British spy and lived out a make-believe tale that swindled seven women and one man out of nearly £1 million pounds. Hendy-Freegard committed his crimes over 10 years during which he claimed that he was a secret service agent being hunted by terrorists. He was such an accomplished liar that he convinced his victims that they too were in danger from terrorist organisations. He persuaded three young students in Shropshire to give up their studies and go on the run with him. Hendy-Freegard told them that he was in danger from an IRA terrorist cell he was investigating. The conman subjected the students to bizarre 'missions' and convinced them to move around the country. He "recruited" the one male student to a bogus spying mission, beat him to "toughen him up", forced him to perform cruel initiation tests, and conned him and his family out of £390,000. He also convinced one of the female students to go on the run with him and incredibly, she spent three weeks the bathroom of her flat hiding from terrorists. While in a relationship with Hendy-Freegard she gave all of her wages to him and he soon conned her family out of £180,000. He lured them away from their families and controlled their contact with the outside world. In many cases, Hendy-Freegard's victims believed they had lost all hope of rejoining normal society. He was finally trapped when the parents of another victim - Kimberley Adams, an American child psychologist - became concerned. They worked with Scotland Yard and the FBI to lure him to Heathrow with the promise of $10,000 if her allowed Kimberley's parents to see her. Once at Heathrow, he was arrested. Unsurprisingly, all of Hendy-Freegard's victims were left so scarred by their experiences that some actually contemplated suicide.

At Blackfriars Crown Court (London) on September 6th 2005 Hendy-Freegard was sentenced to life in prison. The judge in the case told him *"You are an egotistical and opinionated confidence trickster who has shown not a shred of remorse nor compassion for the degradation and suffering to which your victims were subjected"*. Scotland Yard fraud Detective Bob Brandon said that *"In my 25 years as a Detective I've never come across such an accomplished liar. He was just very, very good at spotting people's vulnerabilities, exploiting them and keeping them under his control"*.

Ryley Cruz

In 2016, Ryley Cruz (also using the name Tanya Rowe) conned her victims out of more than £60,000. They included a pub landlord, café owner, several estate agents, property owners, and a waitress who lost her £5000 savings to Cruz. Cruz pretended to be a barrister, a Wonderbra model, a wealthy heiress, a design guru, and a terminally ill cancer patient. She carried around with her a fake CV and numerous forged documents.

For over a decade, Cruz traveled around the country lying and manipulating her (mainly) male victims. Her lies were audacious and persistent. On one occasion Cruz even pretended to be a wealthy heiress with a £30 million fortune and entered into negotiations to buy a half share in a Premiership Rugby Club. On another occasion she used a dating web site to find a wealthy property developer who she conned £34,000 out of in just a few weeks. Cruz lied that she was a successful High Court Barrister awaiting a £150,000 inheritance but was having 'short-term cash flow problems'. She then convinced her victim to rent out an expensive five bedroom Regency house in Cheltenham for her – on the premise that she would pay him back once her legacy came through. This of course never happened. When the victim made repeated requests to get his money back, Cruz threatened him with violence. Her common strategy when victims tracked her down to get their money back was to pretend to have cancer. On one occasion she even managed to get herself admitted to the John Radcliffe Hospital in Oxford, a specialist hospital for cancer care. The victim in this case says that *'Suddenly, I got a text from her saying she was in hospital having been diagnosed with cancer.'* On reflection, he does not know how she fooled NHS staff. *'It's easy to kick myself for being foolish now but when you see someone lying in a hospital bed, with an oxygen mask and groaning in pain, how could you know that she was conning them too?'* The victim only realized the extent of Cruz' deception when she lied that she was on a witness protection scheme and attempted to recruit one of the victim's own employees to pretend to be a police liason officer- the employee duly informed her boss of this and the scam was revealed. Her victim was devastated at the level of deceit involved, *'I cannot tell you how I felt at that moment,'* he says. *'I realised when I thought that I had been calling the liaison officer, I was calling another phone that belonged to Ryley.'*

Ultimately, Cruz' charge sheet was extensive and she was found guilty of 14 charges of fraud, one of posing as a barrister and two of possessing forged documents in order to commit fraud. She was sentenced to over 5 years in prison, with the judge describing Cruz as *"a practiced and indeed accomplished liar and skilled forger"*. The judge further remarked to Cruz *"you have not shown one ounce of remorse or regret for any of your offences. The word 'sorry' has not been uttered by you once...You are, even by the standards of the criminal courts, exceptionally devious. You played the cancer card at will and you have conned a leading hospital in this country"*.

Mark Acklom

Like Cruz, Mark Acklom had a long record of fraudulent crimes. He became one of the UK's most wanted fugitives after leaving a 62-year old divorcee penniless and suicidal. The lifelong conman posed as a wealthy Swiss banker, property developer and MI6 spy in order to romance Carolyn Woods.

Acklom conned Ms Woods into having a relationship with him in order to steal her life-savings. He led Carolyn to believe that they would get married (Acklom was already married with children) and that the money was going to be used to renovate what would become their marital home. However, Acklom fled with the money (nearly £850,000) to Spain and then onto Switzerland. While Acklom was in Spain he was jailed for a property scam and when released early, fled to Switzerland, where he continued his life of crime by operating a bogus data company.

After a European Arrest Warrant was issued for Acklom in 2016, the National Crime Agency, working alongside Avon & Somerset police and authorities in Switzerland, tracked Acklom down and extradited him back to the UK from Switzerland. When his case was eventually heard at Bristol County Court, Acklom was charged with 8 counts of fraud by false representation and 12 counts of converting criminal property. After pleading guilty to the charges he was sentenced to over 5 years in prison.

The devastation that Acklom's crime left behind was extensive and beyond comprehension. In her victim impact statement to the court Carolyn Woods powerfully articulated the effects of Acklom's malicious deception on her life:

"I have been condemned to a life that I don't want... what I had to get my head around what the fact that the man I fell in love with never actually existed: he was the fictitious creation of Mark Acklom"

She goes on:

"My life as I knew it has indeed been destroyed and it has only been the love of my two daughters that has prevented me from ending it completely"

As a result of Acklom's con Carolyn Woods was left destitute and suffered major financial ruin. After sentencing, the Senior Investigating Officer on the case (Gary Atkins) further highlighted the wickedness of Acklom's crime:

"Mark Acklom is a career criminal and a master manipulator who cared little about the emotional devastation he was leaving in his wake. He carried out a callous romance fraud against Carolyn Woods which ruined her life...on the surface Acklom was charming, affluent and successful. Underneath he was calculating, scheming and obsessive about money. His ability to manipulate knew no bounds...Acklom is without morality when it comes to deception".

Juliette D'Souza

London-based Juliette D'Souza posed as a 'shaman' or spiritual healer in order to con victims out of millions of pounds. A judge described her scam in court as *"the worst confidence fraud that I have ever had to deal with"*. He said D'Souza had case a 'spell' over her victims and 'wrecked their lives' out of 'pure greed'. Her victims included a retired opera singer, the wife of a City financier, as well as a photographer and retired Solicitor. Many of these victims were extremely vulnerable: some had family members with cancer or were dying from cancer them-selves; some were struggling to have children; and others had serious physical problems. Assuming multiple identi-ties to hide her crimes, D'Souza convinced them that if they made 'sacrifice payments' (through her of course) as 'spiritual offering' to a sacred tree in the Amazonian rain-forest, she could cure them of all of their problems. One victim gave D'Souza more than £170,000 in the hope that it would help her conceive. A photographer for the Sunday Times photographer started paying cash to D'Souza in late 2004 to help his mother who was having heart surgery, racking up £43,000 in 'sacrifice' payments. The con woman had told him that 'his mother would die if he didn't pay'. A retired opera singer, hoping to cure her ter-minally ill sister and friend from cancer, was conned out of a total of £353,000. Another, an osteopath, genuinely believed D'Souza had "special powers" and was com-pletely under her influence until he realised it was all a con.

The reality was that there was no 'sacred tree' or spiritual healing. Instead, D'Souza kept all of their money for herself and used it to fund a lavish lifestyle abroad and in the UK. This included purchasing expensive cars, luxury flats and holidays, jewellery, and designer handbags.

In court, D'Souza was sentenced to 10 years in prison for 23 counts of fraud and of obtaining property by deception. Jailing D'Souza, who had previous convictions for dishonesty and deception, the judge was scathing in his judgement of how badly her victims were treated by her, *"...they were terrified in many cases of the consequences of disobeying your instructions. You intimidated them with threats of dreadful consequences should they disobey your instructions. They became entirely dependent on you. To reinforce their dependency on you, you actually saw to it that they were cut off from their own friends and family"*.

D' Souza's elaborate hoax lasted for more than a decade and left many of her victims in financial ruin, resulting in one of her clients losing her home and others on the brink of suicide.

Alistair Stewart

Ex-public schoolboy Alistair Stewart posed as a retired Goldman Sachs billionaire in order to swindle a wealthy divorcee out of more than £600,000. He lied that he had been a successful financier at Goldman Sachs for more than 20 years and claimed that he wanted to buy an island retreat. He contacted Nina Siegenthaler who lived in the Caribbean and worked for Sotheby's International Realty. After romancing Siegenthaler online for six months, Stewart conned her into handing over her life savings on the premise that the money would be invested in companies such as BP.

The reality however, was that Stewart simply used the money to fund his own luxury lifestyle. Once he had her money Stewart spent it within four months on buying top range cars, trips in helicopters and private jets, and stays in luxury hotels. Stewart's employment history was nothing more than a tissue of lies and his entire scam was orchestrated from his bedsit where his only source of income was state benefits.

Stewart pleaded guilty to fraud by false representation and was eventually jailed for five-and-half years at the Old Bailey. Judge Stephen Kramer told Stewart that he had caused his victim *"immense psychological as well as financial harm"*. The Prosecutor in the case (Benn Maguire) said that Stewart had been *"adept at targeting victims who were emotionally vulnerable and manipulating their weaknesses to his financial and personal advantage and persuading them to dance to his particular tune"*. Nina Siegenthaler herself was scathing of the damage Stewart had caused her. Speaking in the Evening Standard newspaper she said: *"He is a cunning predator- a man without conscience or moral compass, someone who draws people to him not just to steal their money but to steal their self-worth and dignity. I personally have experienced a profound sense of violation on many levels. I want to underscore the seriousness of the shock and trauma that resulted from this deception. His insatiable desire to dupe leaves a path of destruction in its wake"*

Ivan Nkazi

In 2019 ex-footballer Ivan Nkazi was found guilty of 20 counts of fraud and jailed for three years. Nkazi used the dating sites 'Tinder', 'Plenty of Fish', and 'Bumble' to con several women out of huge sums of money over a four-year period. He set up false dating profiles on each of the sites and used several aliases and photographs. Nkazi pretended to be a well-known American basketball player in order to make initial contact with the women and even set up a detailed indexing system at his home so that he could keep track of the background stories that he was telling each of them, their names, their phone numbers, and the particular dating site that he had used to contact them on. To maintain his lies, Nkazi would use information about his own personal life and children but would change more intimate details in order to avoid getting caught. One of his victims (an investment banker) withdrew money on three separate occasions for him, transferring £1,500 to Nkazi in just one day. He constantly pressurized her for increasing amounts of money. Commonly with each victim, Nkazi would arrange a date but then when she was on her way to meet him, he would claim that his car had broken down and that he needed immediate cash. On other occasions he would use convincing sob stories to manipulate the women into giving him larger sums of money. When any of his victims failed to give him money, things would turn nasty and Nkazi would threaten them with violence. 'In one text message he sent he vowed to attack the woman with acid if she did not pay him the money he was demanding. The text (later revealed court) said: *"I will f*** you up. I will kill your dad...acid in your face, I will come to that address, police or anything, I don't give a f***"*. When police eventually visited NKazi's home to investigate the frauds, they found several mobile phones, including one that had the contact details of more than 100 women.

After sentencing Nkazi Judge Trevor Jones described the conman's threats as 'menacing and ugly', arguing that he took *"advantage of women's vulnerability and naivety, to exploit them and extract significant sums of money."*

The Detective Sergeant in charge of the case summed up the depths of Nkazi's manipulation and greed:

"Nkazi defrauded his victims when he contacted them through dating websites pretending to be someone else. Here, he would blackmail and even threaten some victims into paying him large sums of money. All the time, never having any intention of engaging in a real relationship with them. He is also reported to have threatened to throw acid in some victim's faces, turn up at their work and harm their families...Nkazi is a cruel human being who manipulated countless women for his own financial gain. He clearly had no respect for those he was speaking to and tricked them into thinking he had feelings for them. I hope he takes this time to reflect on the emotional and financial torment he has inflicted on these women"

While the cases of Hendy-Freegard, Cruz, Acklom, D'Souza, Stewart, and Nkazi may be seen as far-fetched examples of the ways in which 'normal' individuals can be taken in by preposterous lies, the cases are real as are the devastating consequences of these frauds on their victims. In the examples discussed above, victims have suffered the loss of huge sums of money. Victims have also been left psychologically damaged and many confidence frauds go unreported because those affected are simply too embarrassed and ashamed to publicly admit that they have been duped.

In the case of Linsey Cotton in Scotland, her con clearly had truly tragic consequences beyond monetary loss-directly leading as it did to the deaths of two innocent women in the most horrendous of circumstances. Margaret and Nicola killed themselves in a budget hotel because they simply could see no other way out of the dreadful situation they believed they were in. They were two completely innocent women who were taken in by Cotton's manipulative games.

The incredible torment felt by both women prior to their deaths must have been extreme. Margaret and Nicola drove to a small town on the West Coast of Scotland knowing that they were intending to end their lives in the most traumatic of ways. They did this because of Linsey Cotton's lies and her manipulation of Michael McDonough as a catalyst to their desperate actions. Margaret and Nicola wanted to help their son and brother out of a situation that they thought that he was in and were devastated when they believed that their actions had made his situation worse.

The Cotton case and the deaths of Margaret and Nicola McDonough lead to a key question: would we all have fallen for such a con? In the other cases of manipulation outlined in this book, would we all have become victims? Given Cotton's expertise in spinning tales, would we too have believed her lies? At face value, Cotton's tales of a brain-injured girlfriend, bogus drug trials and a government cover up, seem incredulous. Why would the McDonough's have believed what, on the surface, were clearly fantastical tales? Cotton was an accomplished liar and adept at manipulating those around her. As her ex partner Gordon Johnstone attested, Cotton was no stranger to exploiting people in order to gain financially and emotionally from them. But how precisely was Linsey Cotton able to manoeuvre the McDonough family so expertly? How did she distract them from asking serious questions about the outlandish stories that she was telling them? Why did Michael and his family not see through her preposterous lies?

Chapter 9:

Online Con Artists and Can We All Become Victims?

This book does not make the claim that Linsey Cotton was a master con artist and criminal. Instead, it argues that she was a good liar and manipulator. Advances in technology over the last 30 years have undoubtedly made the job of confidence tricksters like Cotton much easier. With the introduction of the internet and the advent of email and online messaging, we are all regularly bombarded with 'phishing' scams, spam messages, and unsolicited 'friend' requests on social media sites. For fraudsters, these communications are cheap and quick to send out. Many con artists carry out their deceptions using mobile phones and laptop computers. Linsey Cotton used these technologies to maximum effect in her manipulation of the McDonough family-initially contacting Michael McDonough using a fake profile on a popular online dating site. Over several months Cotton bombarded Michael with thousands of online messages. She then used a number of mobile phones and computers to pretend to be various people in 'Steph's' life. Without these technologies Cotton's task would have undoubtedly been much more difficult.

Before the Internet, con artists committing 'romance' frauds would often find their victims in the personal ads of magazines. Technology has however streamlined communication and given fraudsters, like Cotton, the opportunity to target much larger pools of victims in a co-ordinated way. In Cotton's case it is not clear how many people she contacted online before Michael McDonough became her victim. Online dating sites (like 'Plenty of Fish') give scammers access to several victims at the same time, making it easier to target them with online messages and demands. If one potential victim does not take the bait fraudsters can easily move on to another. This ease of communication might help to explain why someone would willingly hand over money and gifts to a stranger that they had only talked to by computer. Michael McDonough for example, gave Linsey Cotton cash and presents long before he had even set eyes on her. In a revealing statement, Michael told police that her intricate web of lies "*all made sense to him at the time.*" This comment highlights how adept con artists can actually be in persuading their targets to believe that what they are telling them is true given that outside the context of a specific scam, it is difficult to explain actions that seem (to the rest of us) so irrational. However, once you look *inside* the workings of a scam, the responses of victims become much more understandable. Cotton flooded Michael McDonough with numerous texts and emails over a short period of time, telling lie after lie. This meant that Michael had little opportunity to sit back and actually reflect on the story that she was telling him about 'Steph'.

In her 2008 book, *Truth, Lies and Trust* on the Internet, Monica Whitty outlines the mechanics of online relationships. She makes the point that more of our lives are visible online, for example, where we work, how we shop, who we are in a relationship with, where we socialize, and who our friends and contacts are. Computer-mediated relationships, Whitty says, can be "hyperpersonal — more strong and intimate than physical relationships." This is because the online world is relatively anonymous and people can have more control over how they present themselves. However, with this comes the potential for greater duplicity and deception. The internet increases the potential for people to do things that they would never dream of doing offline such as cyber bullying or stalking. In the case of a con artist like Linsey Cotton it allowed her the chance to take on other personas and misrepresent herself in the most audacious ways possible.

At a distance communication such as emails, texts and instant messenger allow criminals to be strategic in the stories they tell and the messages they send, creating the perfect online suitor. In June 2019 for example, a mother of one from Wales became the victim of an online romance fraud to the tune of £40,000. The man who conned her stole the identity of a handsome French national and used his image to create a number of fake profiles on social media sites. He used tales of woe (for example, claiming that he had been robbed) to convince his victim to send him money. In the case of Linsey Cotton, she set up a fake online profile and pretended to be a young, attractive university student to lure her victim in. Victims of romance scams are often so taken in by these fake profiles that they struggle to delete messages and photographs sent to them by the criminal, even after they have been told that they have been scammed. They simply refuse to accept the fact that they have been duped.

Almost every day in the news there are reports of the scams of con artists and confidence tricksters. In 2016 for example, the UK newspaper *The Mirror* reported the case of a 33-year old British businessman (Niall Rice) who paid nearly half a million pounds to two American based psychics to reunite him with a woman that he had briefly met. Love struck Niall Rice says he "just got sucked in" after turning to the fortuneteller who promised him that she could make the women in question love him back. Many reading about these sorts of crimes are often critical of the victims involved, shocked at how people could be so gullible and naive. They argue that they themselves would never be fooled by such cons- in other words, that con's only happen to *other* people. They support the saying's that "If it seems too good to be true it probably is" or the connected saying, "There's no such thing as a free lunch".

Those criticizing fraud victims also assume that those who fall for scams are weak and have certain qualities – that they are uneducated, poor, lonely, elderly, socially isolated, recently bereaved or vulnerable in other ways. Many victims of frauds do indeed possess these traits. In other cases, however the victims are not who you would traditionally think of as 'vulnerable' but are intelligent, professional, street wise, socially aware individuals. Maria Konnikova in her book *"The Confidence Game"*

(Viking, 2016) argues that it is much easier to fall for con's than people think. She makes the important point that even the most intelligent, cynical and skeptical of people *can* be manipulated into believing the most bizarre of lies. Intelligent people can and do behave stupidly.

According to Konnikova (2016) becoming a victim is less to do with intelligence but more about where people are at in particular times in their lives. For example, if they are going through unemployment, divorce, bereavement or debt, then people are naturally more vulnerable to the promises/flattery of smooth talking fraudsters who lie that they will improve their lives or fill any void that they have in their lives at that particular moment.

In this way, it is arguable that **everyone** is a potential victim if the circumstances are right. For Konnikova (2016) a small part of what makes victims believe a scam is their own belief that they are somehow the exception to the rule- that they are more savvy than other people and somehow deserve, for example, a good return on their investment or a lasting loving new relationship.

So, if we accept that even the most skeptical of people can become victims, **how** do confidence artists manipulate their victims? Michael McDonough and his mother and sister were intelligent people who were leading successful happy lives at the time that Cotton entered their world. Michael was an accomplished technician serving in the Royal Air Force. He was obviously using on line dating sights to try and meet a potential partner. His sister Nicola had successfully completed her University degree and was planning a career in social work. Their mother, Margaret McDonough, had fostered a number of children in care for Renfrewshire District Council and twice stood as a Liberal Democratic candidate in the local council elections. The McDonough family as a whole were undoubtedly a successful, middle class family who had achieved a lot and were enjoying living their lives to the full. Linsey Cotton also was living a relatively normal life in Scotland, living not far from the McDonough family and bringing up two children on her own.

So how did someone like Cotton, an ordinary single mother of two children living an everyday, mundane life, take advantage of the McDonough's and construct a story so bizarre and fantastical that three members of the same family were taken in by her and believed her lies?

Chapter 10:

Con Artists, Their Techniques of Persuasion and the 'Dark Triad'

Konnikova (2016) in *"The Confidence Game"* makes the point that in everyday life, most of us carry out what she calls 'micro cons' - small lies or deceptions designed to either make a friend feel better, protect ourselves, cover for a colleague, or bolster a friendship or association. Significantly however, what differentiates this 'micro con' from the con artists described in this book is the *nefarious intent* of the scammer. Nefarious refers to actions that are essentially wicked, sinful and immoral. What this means is that scammers and fraudsters are **never** motivated by 'good' intensions but instead are always driven by self-serving, cruel, greedy objectives. Con artists have no compassion for their victims but have only an 'end game' in sight that motivates all of their actions towards achieving the goals of their con. The 'end game' commonly involves exhorting as much money and goods as possible from the victim/s, with minimal effort or cost to themselves.

The first stage of any deception is what is referred to as the 'put-up' or *identifying a victim*. As Konnikova

(2016) has argued, even the most intelligent and skeptical of people can become the victim of a con artist. It has already been mentioned that becoming the victim of a con artist is less about intelligence or being too trusting than **where someone is at a particular time in their life.** The literature is clear that divorce, separation, loneliness, bereavement, unemployment, debt and financial strain can lower people's defenses and increase the chance of them becoming the victim of a con. Experiencing some sort of life turmoil or strain at any particular time in any of our lives can make us more vulnerable to someone who wants to take advantage. This is because being vulnerable is often associated with a reduced ability to resist exploitation and conversely, an increased tendency to being emotionally or physically abused. Con artists are especially good at sensing the vulnerability of their victims and capitalizing on it.

For Konnikova (2016) this first stage of a con (the 'put up') is the most intuitive in that it strongly relies on the 'skill' of the fraudster in actually 'reading' their victim and taking note of their views, personality traits and self-perceptions.

In the case of Michael McDonough, one can surmise that he was initially on the 'Plenty of Fish' dating website because he was looking for company or to start some sort of romantic relationship (online or otherwise). Michael was initially targeted by Cotton on the dating website because he was (1) lured in by the very attractive profile picture used by Cotton and (2) apparently lonely while working on board a rather isolated navel base in a remote part of Scotland. Michael was working away from his family and friends and would have no doubt welcomed some pleasant social contact. Cotton seemed to quickly detect Michael's vulnerabilities and made her move. Similarly with Michael's mother and sister (Nicola and Margaret), both had emotional vulnerabilities that made them more likely to be victims of Cotton's cruel manipulation. Nicola was known to suffer from depression and her mum Margaret was still seen as emotionally frail after the end of her 28-year long marriage. It is important to stress that these factors in **no way** apportion any form of 'blame' or highlight any personality 'flaws' of the victims but simply serve to highlight the brazeiness of con men and woman in abusing the real vulnerabilities of people at certain times in their lives. Crucially, Nicola and Margaret were also very caring individuals who wanted to do everything in their power to help out their brother/son. Linsey Cotton was good at manipulating people. In saying this it is still important to keep in mind that although Cotton was no Mark Acklom- she was no international criminal master mind- she was a good liar.

The second key stage of any con is the *building of familiarity and trust*. Individuals are naturally more likely to trust those who feel familiar to them. Building this rapport or familiarity is deceptive because it often leads victims to believe that **they** are the ones in control- and this is what the fraudster intends. 'Confidence games' are often called as such because the whole premise of the confidence game is that fraudsters ask for the 'confidence' of their victims and their victims freely give it to them. As Konnikova argues (2016) *"There is nothing a con artist likes to do than make us feel* *powerful…that we are the ones calling the shots, making the choices, doing the thinking"*. Con artists achieve this control, not through overt violence or force but through more subtle forms of persuasion.

For Konnikova (2016) the perfect con is an exercise in what she calls **soft skills**. These soft skills are more insidious that outright physical control in that con artists rarely force anyone to do anything but use persuasion, influence and trust to get what they want. Crucially, these soft skills can override the judgement and intelligence of victims.

In the case of Linsey Cotton, it is clear that she possessed soft skills in abundance, rarely having to resort to physical violence to manipulate her victims. She seems to have been particularly good at spinning a range of tales and getting her victims to believe the lies that she was telling them. She had a long history of lying and manipulating her victims to get what she wanted. In the case of her ex-partner Gordon Johnstone for example, Cotton initially lured him into a relationship through complete bravado and guile. Pretending to be 'Steph' (again), Cotton lied to Johnstone that 'Steph' had been involved in a serious car accident and persuaded him to stay with her overnight in order to 'comfort her'. Once she got him to move in with her, Cotton then persuaded Johnstone to give up his job and then slowly starting using her influence to cut him off from his friends and family. These are all examples of 'soft skills' where the perpetrator of the con is very adept at manouvering their victims into action which ultimately serves to **only** benefit the perpetrator. These actions are met with little resistance from the victim because the con man or woman has actually got the victim to **believe** in their own minds that for example, not contacting their friends or family is a good thing. This is a powerful skill indeed and is a skill that Linsey Cotton seems to have possessed in abundance.

Cotton initially developed a connection with Michael McDonough through endless hours of online conversations, allowing Michael to talk and to share details of his family and job. Over several months these lengthy conversations quickly built up rapport and trust between them both. Michael trusted what Cotton was saying to him and clearly believed that his relationship with 'Steph' was real. He had no reason to believe otherwise. Cotton always presented a positive image of herself (and her association with 'Steph') and used this to deceive Michael into believing that she was a trustworthy, reliable person. She took advantage of the information that Michael told her about his family and used it to shape her scheme. None of this information was gained with violence but with cunning and duplicity.

In the case of all of the other con artists discussed in this book (for eg. Mark Acklom, Ryley Cruz, Robert Hendy-Freegard), it is clear that they too possessed 'soft skills' in abundance. Mark Acklom was particularly skilled at taking on various guises and manipulating those around him. Acklom pretended to be a rich Swiss banker and an MI6 agent, before defrauding his ex-girlfriend out of her entire life savings. Acklom's victim described his 'silver tongue' and ability to persuade her into a relationship after only knowing her a short time. After claiming that he had cash flow problems, his ex-girlfriend began transferring money into Acklom's bank account-believing that the money was being used to help fund a house renovation project. In reality, Acklom was using her money to finance his lavish lifestyle of fast cars, exotic holidays and expensive homes.

What Acklom seems to have been especially good at was building rapport quickly (especially with women) and then manipulating the belief of his victims that the scheme or scenario they are being included in, is a mutually beneficial one. No violence or physical threats are used. Instead victims are manipulated using emotional exploitation and mental distortion. These tactics are designed to seize power and control at the expense of victims. In many ways individuals like Mark Acklom and Linsey Cotton are good at brainwashing their victims into believing that the story they are being told is 'real' and 'true'. In the case of Acklom, his story centered on his mysterious lifestyle as an MI6 agent and tax-exiled Swiss-based banker. Similarly, Linsey Cotton told lie after lie and even though Michael McDonough may have been suspicious of her lies, he continued to go along with her scheme.

The third key stage of any deception is *implementing the con*. Once trust has been established and rapport built, the wheels of the con are put into motion. This may mean the con artist weighing up in more detail what can be gained from the victim and the precise means of achieving this. Putting the con into motion also means building upon the basis of trust and familiarity that has already been established with the victim. It also commonly means getting the victim to 'buy into' the tale or story that has been told to them by the con artist. These tales are often designed to court sympathy for the fraudster and their so-called dire predicament. In the case of Linsey Cotton, her 'story' was a bizarre one: revolving around as it did the mysterious 'Steph', her poor health and her treatment at the hands of a rather shady medical testing agency called 'Biotech Scotland'. Michael was already highly emotionally invested in 'Steph' by this point and believed that they were in a serious relationship engaged to be married. This meant that he was easily manipulated into providing the resources- through Cotton- needed to 'save' 'Steph'. It is arguable that even if Michael had any doubts at this stage about the story Cotton was telling him, he was so emotionally invested in Cotton's tale that he would have found it difficult to extricate himself. Margaret and Nicola McDonough in turn, became invested in Cotton's story precisely because Michael was so embroiled and they desperately wanted to help him.

While Cotton's fraud was principally driven by money, there is some element of her crime that fulfilled deeper motives. She clearly wanted male attention. She felt the need to use a false identity online because she had little confidence that her own appearance would attract men. She also used an image of a woman who she believed Michael (or most men) would be attracted to.

The final stage of any con is the 'blow off' or end game. The end stage of any con usually involves the perpetrator of the crime disappearing from the scene after taking all that they can from their victim. The fraudster then often relies on the victim being slow to react or being so shocked at what has happened to them, that they delay in reporting the crime to the police. In online romance frauds in particular, victims are often too ashamed or embarrassed by the fact that they have been taken in by a potential love interest, that they do not report the crime to the authorities. In many cases the fraudster is long gone and out of the scene before the con even comes to light. Konnikova (2016) is clear that con artists are often aware that most people will **not** report the crime because they do not want to ruin their reputations. She goes on *"Our reputation is the most important thing we have. It determines not only how we are seen by others, but also how they will act toward us...that is precisely what the confidence artist is counting on, even after, despite our best efforts at self-delusion, it becomes apparent that we've been taken for a ride: that our reputational motivation will be strong enough to keep us quiet. In the touch, we've finally been taken for all we've had: the grafter has gotten all he's after".*

In Cotton's case, it is interesting that she did **not** disappear from the scene when she had got money and goods from Michael McDonough, but hung around. Even when she had pressured Michael's mother and sister into suicide, she did not flee the scene but remained at Michael's side, even when Nicola was brought into hospital with severe wounds.

So what makes a good con artist? While it is difficult to generalize about the standard personality 'type' of con artists, most possess what psychologists call the *"dark triad of traits"*. These traits are described as 'dark' because they are all underpinned by spiteful, uncaring, evil motives. Not all individuals who possess these traits become fraudsters and con artists. These traits can also be found in lawyers, politicians and businessmen. Neither do con artists necessarily possess *all* three of the dark triad of traits and each trait has a different focus. The common factor however, is that all three involve people who put themselves first in order to get what they want. The 'dark triad' refers to the three negative personality traits of **psychopathy**, **narcissism**, and **Machiavellianism**.

According to Konnikova in *"The Confidence Game"* (Viking, 2016) most successful con artists have a large degree of psychopathy to their personalities. On the positive side, psychopaths can, on the surface be, extremely charming and likeable people. On the negative side however, psychopaths are pathological liars who lack empathy and remorse. While they may be able to **mimic** emotions, they are not capable of genuinely caring for another person. As a result, those with psychopathic personalities find it difficult to establish meaningful personal relationships. In the context of a con, this means that they are emotionally 'empty' and not able to empathize with the plight of their victims. Due to the fact that psychopaths process emotional stimuli differently, they see little value in the individuals they are conning and therefore are not emotionally engaged in the pain they are causing another person. Psychopaths can exploit and manipulate others easily precisely because they lack empathy and feel no remorse.

In the case of Linsey Cotton, it is clear that her psychopathy manifested itself in the constant lies that she told throughout her relationships and in the lack of empathy for the pain that she was causing people- particularly, the McDonough family. Even when she was caught, Cotton did not express any genuine remorse for the fact that as a direct result of her actions, two innocent women were dead. A chilling fact to emerge out of research for this book is that Cotton was actually with Michael McDonough at the hospital when his sister was brought in severely injured. She was at Michael McDonough's side, pretending to be supportive and feigning distress and upset in front of his family - when she clearly felt nothing.

Closely linked to the psychopathic trait in con artists is their narcissism. Narcissists are always driven by what they want and what they believe they *deserve* that they should have.

Successful con men and women tend to have an overblown impression of their worth- seeing themselves as better, more intelligent, and more deserving than those around them. Narcissists believe themselves to be superior to those around them and desire attention, admiration and praise. If they ever face criticism or views that do not match their own, they get extremely defensive, and dismissive. Narcissists are arrogant and have a strong sense of entitlement, believing that they are more deserving than other people. They are extremely selfish and do not like to see others succeed. They will happily lie, cheat and steal in order to get ahead and make themselves feel good.

Narcissists also tend to be bored by routine and are always on the look out for new challenges. Individuals who possess strong narcissistic traits often do not want to work hard for rewards but constantly look for are shortcuts to get what they want. Becoming a con artist is a perfect way for narcissists to get financial gain with minimal effort.

In addition to their psychopathy and narcissism, con artists also have Machiavellian traits. Machiavellianism is always about manipulation for personal gain. Someone Machiavellian is often described as cunning, sneaky, and lacking a moral compass. Those with Machiavellian personality types are master manipulators and are good at convincing others that what they are saying is true. They have poor emotional attachments to other people and regularly exploit and deceive others to get what they want. Due to the fact that they feel no empathy, they have no feelings about what they are doing to another person (they just do not care) and so do not feel that they are doing anything wrong.

Despite sharing characteristics with the other 'dark traits' of narcissism and psychopathy, Machiavellianism is also a distinctive trait on its own. Whereas narcissists and psychopaths can be charming and engage with others on some form of superficial social level (serial killer Ted Bundy being a classic example of this), Machiavellians are less likely to engage with others socially and instead, rely on their own thinking and planning to get what they want. Machiavellians are therefore more withdrawn than psychopaths and narcissists. This fits entirely with their profile as being cold, calculating individuals who strategically plot against others in order to achieve their goals.

Linsey Cotton clearly had Machavellian tendencies and kept her scheme going even when she must have known the great distress her scheming and lies were causing the McDonough family. As mentioned already, she was at the hospital when Nicola McDonough was admitted gravely ill, yet she still managed to feign distress and concern in front of both Michael and his family. This clearly takes a personality with strong self-preserving tendencies to carry this off.

Summary and Conclusions

The callous actions of con men and woman litter the news on a daily basis. Hardly a day goes by when we fail to read about the deceptions carried out by con artists, scammers and romance fraudsters. As this book has demonstrated, the consequences of these crimes are catastrophic for the victims involved. In many cases, victims loose their homes, life savings, goods, and importantly, their confidence and self-belief. Many are so ashamed and embarrassed by what has happened to them that they don't report the crime to the authorities. Fraudsters rely on this fact and have no empathy for the distress and pain they have caused their victims. Con artists are expert manipulators and can walk away with no conscience about the devastation they have left behind. As Konnikova (2016) argues, most con artists have psychopathic traits in their personalities and so, while on the surface they may appear charming and sociable, underneath they are lone 'sharks'- pathological, narcissistic liars who feel no remorse or empathy for those they are manipulating. Sadly, the Linsey Cotton's, Mark Acklom's, and Robert Hendy-Freegard's of this world are always operating amongst us, looking for their next 'target'.

The case of Nicola and Margaret McDonough is a truly sad one. Linsey Cotton undoubtedly took advantage of their loving and trusting natures and along with their son (and brother) Michael, used the family to fulfill her need for both attention and money. The story that she told the family- about the mysterious 'Steph'- was an undeniably ludicrous one but was one that they all believed to be true. Although Cotton was certainly no Mark Acklom (in the sense that her deceptions were never on a grand, international scale like his involving the creation of large companies and vast sums of money) Cotton possessed some expertise in deception and lying. Through constant communication with Michael McDonough, Cotton manipulated him into believing that what she was telling him about 'Steph' and her treatment at the hands of Biotech Scotland, was true. His mother and sister had the best interests of Michael at heart and simply wanted to help him out of the desperate situation they believed he was in. What they didn't know, of course, was that Linsey Cotton was an experienced liar and had used the 'Steph' scenario before to manipulate a previous partner (Gordon Johnstone). In reality, there was no girlfriend called 'Steph', no medical company called 'Biotech Scotland' and no confidentiality agreement. They were all figments of Cotton's vivid imagination, designed to gain her both male attention and money. Michael McDonough had been duped as had his mother and sister. They all believed her bizarre lies and were taken in by the story that she had created. It seems incredulous that Cottons scam took place over a short 9-month period but led to such a horrendous life-changing conclusion for the whole McDonough family.

The fact that Linsey Cotton died in prison (from natural causes) while only 6 months into her sentence for defrauding the McDonough's in no way mitigates the utter devastation that she left behind. As a direct result of her deception and manipulation, Nicola and Margaret McDonough took their own lives in the most horrendous of circumstances. They did this because they were desperate and believed that there was no other way out of the situation they were in. Rather than face 20 years of imprisonment, they drove from their home in Paisley to a budget hotel on the West Coast of Scotland and ended their own lives. The complete depths of despair that they both must have felt would have been powerful and overwhelming. In their mindset at that particular time in their lives, Nicola and Margaret would have believed that killing themselves would end their suffering and also not worsen the situation that they believed Michael McDonough was in around the (non existent) Biotech 'confidentiality agreement'.

It is arguable that while Linsey Cotton could not have reasonably foreseen that her lies would have directly led to the deaths of the two women, their deaths were undoubtedly a direct consequence of her actions. For that, Cotton without doubt, committed what can be correctly described as 'the cruellest con'.

This book is respectfully dedicated to the memory of Nicola and Margaret McDonough. May they both rest in peace.

Lightning Source UK Ltd.
Milton Keynes UK
UKHW021043050220
358194UK00009B/129

9 781839 750076